THE PROCESSION

THE
PROCESSION

BY

KHALIL GIBRAN

Edited, translated, and
with a biographical sketch by
George Kheirallah

PHILOSOPHICAL LIBRARY
New York

TO THE SONS AND DAUGHTERS
OF LEBANON

THE PROCESSION

CONTENTS

The Life of
Gibran Khalil Gibran

WITH its shores caressed by the warm, indigo blue waters of the Mediterranean Sea, its lofty peaks turbaned with perpetual snow, the hoary and sacred Lebanon basks meditatively under the sunny, rarified skies of Mother Syria.

Nations were born on its western slopes; others were nursed and sheltered by it in the Orontes valley, and civilizations sprouted and matured in the not distant Plains of Shinar, under its watchful and benevolent eye. Although it lacked comparative fertility, the dwellers of its slopes were compensated by a plentiful supply of hardy cedar, planted there by the hand of God.

Its inhabitants built boats, sailed seas, and furnished their only available wealth to Egypt in the south and to the valley of the Euphrates on the east. The caskets of the

Pharaohs within the sarcophagi, the beams of the Temples, the doors and furnishings, all required this precious wood. Their seamanship made the Phoenicians the world's foremost traders and civilizers. Their greatest gifts, however, were not cedar, weaves, purple dyes, glass or metal castings (nor even their alphabet and sculptures which they bore to the then untutored Greeks and Romans), but rather the moral and spiritual revelations which their poets, seers, and prophets gave to the world.

For was it not in Lebanon that Tammuz was born? Did he not roam these very hills? Did he not descend to the depth of its valleys to cut and fashion his own reed and ascend again to scale its highest crags to play and sing? Beautiful of face, free of limb, and bold of spirit, he ranged the hillside, rode the wings of its tempests, communed with its stars and was lulled to sleep by the rustling of the leaves of its forests. Here the gentle zephyrs awakened him to plunge again into its crystalline rivers, quaff its water, and race its gazelles and antelopes, with

Ishtar (Venus) in pursuit of this God of
Beauty and Youth.

For many centuries the maidens of the
Lebanon gathered on a certain spring day,
adorned themselves in their finest raiment,
bedecked themselves with flowers and orna-
ments, and roamed the hills for hyacinth,
lilies, narcissi, and all the flowers with which
the gods have especially carpeted the Leba-
non. These they brought in armfuls to the
River of Tammuz where, forming them-
selves into clusters and groups, they sang,
danced, and bemoaned his death. They
sprinkled their flower offerings on the rip-
pling waters and the little virgins brought
their small bronze statuettes of Tammuz to
throw in the deep pools, hoping that a
Tammuz-like bridegroom might come to
seek them on some future spring day.

Tammuz, like everyone born on the slopes
of these mountains, loved his native land,
and could never resist its charm in spring-
time. Even after he was taken away by
the Greeks, like many of the Syrian gods,
and given the name of Adonis, he always de-

serted Mt. Olympus in springtime and returned to course over his native hills. Many a lovelorn maiden, who kept a vigil between the false and the true dawn, had a glimpse of the handsome Adonis fleeting over a promontory, running into the forest, or diving into the river. Even in our day, watchful shepherds have seen him in the environs of the Sacred Cedars, and many are those who believe that he will be reborn among them.

Wadi-Quadisha (The Holy or Sacred Valley) is the name by which this valley has been reverently called for unknown centuries. No other word could have described the feeling of the beholder than Wadi-Quadisha. The river course today, named Abu-Ali, which empties its waters into the infinite blue near Tripoli, leads towards its source in a steadily mounting grade. After following its upward zigzagging and tortuous course through the foothills and middle mountains, the traveler is suddenly ushered into a hushed and mystic canyon which expands into a basin-like valley, basking in peace and solitude, guarded on either side by immense,

sheer and gigantic ledges of limestone and buttressed at the upper end against the snow-clad mountain.

In the distance, along the rim of the valley, are clusters of stone houses, clinging to the mountainside and forming the few scattered villages of Wadi-Quadisha. This Sacred Valley differs from other parts of the Lebanon because of its abundant water and its verdant and numerous groves of trees. Walnut and oak, zeizaphon, (Ziziphus Spina Christi), poplar and willow trees dot the landscape; graceful and airy pines interspace it here and there, and its terraced slopes are planted with mulberry, fig, fruit trees, and extensive vineyards.

It was to this spot in the early days of Christianity, when the strife of the sects was intense and bitter, that the monk-priest, Mar-Maroon (St. Maroon) came. It was here that his followers increased, and it was here that the Sons of Lebanon, conforming to his teachings, adopted for their ritual, still in use today, the Aramaic language which was spoken by Jesus. Although this church is affil-

iated with the Roman Catholic Church, its priests marry and raise families, and its liturgy and ecclesiastical chant—one of the most musical of all—is still followed in the language commanded by Mar-Maroon.

The ascending traveler looking across the white-turbaned mountain facing him may liken this fruitful valley to the chest of an imaginary giant, under whose venerable chin the most ancient and sacred grove of cedars, like a beard, has survived the centuries. A short distance below the cedars, and slightly to the right, seemingly clinging to space, is the typical Lebanon town of Bcherri, the birthplace of Gibran Khalil Gibran.

These Lebanon towns are composed of compactly built homes, constructed of stones, beamed with pine logs, and ceilinged with stone slabs over which earth and gravel are so packed as to make a flat, waterproof roof. After a heavy rain or a snowfall, a smooth stone roller (Mehdela), drawn by wooden pincers fitted into grooved ends, is rolled forward and back over the roof to pack the layer of earth and prevent seepage.

These homes consist of a stone cellar under one or two very large single or double rooms, averaging fifteen by twenty-five feet, to twenty by forty feet, the wider rooms having more pillars to support the visible beams. The walls are plastered with a whitewashed tufta.Towards the back part of this community room in which the family lives, is found a row of built-in provision bins. These are also constructed of tufta, with semi-elliptical openings at the top and a cylindrical outlet about four inches in diameter at the bottom, each of which is closed with a handmade cloth plug. In the fall of the year the wheat, lentils, chick-peas, flour, crushed wheat, and such staple provisions go into their separate bins to be drawn from below by the good housewife. Three or more earthenware jars containing oil, grape molasses, and olives are placed on stands along the wall. The family is thus ready to face a winter of cold weather and social activities.

The beds, quilts and bedding are neatly folded in the morning and placed in a niche alcove to be spread on the floor at sleeping

time. The floor is a crusted packed red clay, polished to a patent-leather shine, which is covered by a matting in summer and by black goat-hair rugs in winter. There are usually two or three small windows set in the wall. The door of heavy wood swings on its oaken pegs into stones grooved above and below. The key, consisting of a piece of wood to which a number of nails are adjusted so as to fit into specific grooves, gave birth to our Yale lock and keys. The hearth is utilized in winter time for cooking and heating purposes, and, as it lacks a chimney, the wood smoke floats to the ceiling to blacken the beams and slabs and escape through a vent high in the wall. While the homes of the well-to-do are spacious and artistic the house in which Gibran Khalil Gibran was born was a modest one.

The people of these villages live on the Baraka, or blessings. They have to terrace into the eroded mountainside in order to reclaim and conserve a bit of fertility for a tree or vine. Their produce is negligible and their season short; yet, in spite of their poverty

and the sterility of their mountain, their towns are as clean as their mountain air, their homes are spotless, their earthen floors are polished twice weekly, and cleanliness, contentment and hospitality are their heritage.

During the early nineties, tales of Eldorado had percolated through the Lebanon hills and were recounted by the mountaineers around their winter hearths. It was said that in America across the sea immigrants were hospitably received regardless of faith or nationality, that the wages paid were in dollars instead of piastres, and that opportunities for gain were plentiful. Some of the poor youth of Bcherri left this peaceful village, bade farewell to their people and the Sacred Cedars and bravely sailed to the Promised Land. These immigrants prospered beyond their fathers' dreams. They sent back dollars which, translated into thousands of piastres, repaid their passage money with interest and provided passage money for their relatives. The children of Phoenicia could not resist the venture.

In 1895 the Gibran family consisted of Khalil, the fair-complexioned, strongly knit, gay father; very fond of his cigarettes, Arabian coffee and an occasional "tear" of native arrak; the dark, slender mother with sensitive features and a wistful Leonardo Da Vinci countenance, daughter of a Maronite priest; her son, Peter, by a former marriage; the boy, Gibran, then twelve years old; and two younger daughters, Mariana and Sultana.

In that year Peter became eighteen and was chafing to go to America to help lighten the load for the jolly and dashing step-father whom he had learned to love; but the mother, whose family name was Rahma (meaning compassion), could not part with her first-born.

Good news and dollars continued to reach Bcherri as evidence of the opportunities in Eldorado, and the mother at last consented to take her children, under the leadership of Peter, to the New World, while her husband remained to care for the small property.

Arriving in the United States, they went directly to Boston where other natives of

Bcherri had settled. There the little Syrian colony had congregated in and around Hudson Street, near Boston's Chinatown. Here the family found a welcome from their townsfolk as well as from other friendly Syrians. The ambitious Peter secured immediate employment, and his mother and the little family danced for joy when he brought back his first pay—figured in piastres it was unbelievable! The mother and the young daughters, with the help of other Syrians and of their needles, soon found work.

"Peter," said his mother, "we must give the little brother the chance denied you. We must educate him to become a great man."

And so Gibran Khalil Gibran, a delicate boy with chestnut hair, high forehead and large, wondering eyes—and here one must stop in describing Gibran—for those large, limpid eyes transported from the wonders of Lebanon, now full of the wonders of the New World, arrested the attention of the beholder so that observation seldom went beyond them—was sent to a public school with young Americans from all nations. The

family plunged into its work with zest. What matter if they missed the high-ceilinged home, rarified air of the cedars, the clear and refreshing mountain streams, the crystalline waters of the Spring of Bcherri, the azure skies of Syria and the distant view of the blue Mediterranean? This dark room, the creaking stairs and the traffic noises which replaced the song of the waterfalls of Wadi-Quadisha were secondary, for their denial now was for the betterment of the family fortune.

Peter now was doing well and was about to have his own little store; the girls would eventually marry; but Gibran was the center of their hopes. Gibran should not follow in the steps of the easy-going shepherd father, he should receive an education. He was different from other children, for in two years in public school he had actually learned to speak English and to read American books.

"May the Saints preserve him!" exclaimed his mother in wonder.

His teacher at school, who took a great interest in this Lebanon boy, had suggested

that he abbreviate his name from Gibran Khalil Gibran to Khalil Gibran, and by this name he became known to his American friends.

During the two years of hard work the frugal family had prospered. In exchange for the life of Baraka or blessing enjoyed by the poor mountaineers, they had accumulated a little fortune in piastres, and their dream of educating their little boy came nearer realization. Peter insisted upon sending the youngster back to Syria, where he was enrolled in the Maronite School at Beyrut to study his native tongue, the Arabic, as well as French.

During vacation time his father, who had been receiving continued assistance from Peter, took the young boy camping in the mountains and visited with him many ruins of olden times. Once again this young fawn of the Lebanon roamed the hills, quenched his thirst at its mountain springs, plucked the dew-drenched clusters of grapes from its vineyards, and inhaled the fragrance of pine and cedar.

His mind opened; undefined thoughts and emotions welled and surged through his being. While basking in the tempered sunshine his thoughts often traveled back to the tenement in Edinburgh Street, to Peter, struggling to build the family fortune; to the bent heads and nimble fingers plying the needle in order that he, Gibran, might have a better chance in life.

Gibran was a boy of moods as he later became a man of moods and during these spells he often sought the Monastery of Mar-Sarkis. In this deserted old monastery, in a sheltered nook of the Sacred Valley, he spent many hours building hopes for the repayment and future comfort of his family. He was going back to America where he would become a great artist and when he had earned money and brought back his mother and sisters to a more comfortable home in Bcherri, he would purchase for himself this deserted Monastery of Mar-Sarkis and make it the cloister and home of his dreams.

Gibran returned to America, after four years of study, and although he made his

mark here, he was never again destined to see the Sacred Valley or his native hills. After his death in the prime of life his only remaining relative, his good sister, Mariana, took him back and reposed his body in this old and peaceful monastery.

Upon his return to Boston he found that little Sultana had died on April 4, 1902. Her frail body preyed upon by the unseen host of tuberculosis, freed her soul to wander back to the flowery fields of Wadi-Quadisha and perchance to drop a blossom into the River of Tammuz. Shortly after his arrival his mother was taken to a hospital suffering from the same plague. The glorious homecoming of this bewildered boy found him even more bewildered. A short time later, as Gibran sat as though stunned, Peter mounted the creaking stairs and flung the door open. He seemed in great distress; his face was flushed with fever and his breathing was labored. It suddenly dawned upon Gibran that the sturdy Peter, who had been the cheerful breadwinner of the family, was now anything but sturdy. Peter told Gibran

that he felt ill; that this tenement must be cursed by unseen disease; that Gibran must desert it and save himself and Mariana. Gibran hastened for a physician who declared Peter in the last stages of consumption. Peter died in March, 1903, and the mother died in the hospital in June of the same year.

Gibran with Mariana left the plague-ridden house and sought a more cheerful home in the neighborhood, where Mariana insisted upon sewing to keep her beloved brother at his art studies. Gibran was keenly conscious of his loneliness and felt that the family's ambition for his advancement was responsible for their bereavement. He blamed himself and suffered agonies of remorse, rebelling against Mariana's labors and sacrifices, but Mariana pleaded that by following the path of advancement which his mother and brother had so wished for him Gibran would be fulfilling a sacred duty to their memory.

Grief and agony laid its stamp on this hypersensitive boy throughout his life. It opened chasms of problems and questions

before him; it extended his vista into the Empyrean, heightened his sense of color and attuned his subconsciousness to the most delicate light and shade, and welled his springs of sympathy and tenderness. Isaiah's eloquence mingled with Jeremiah's sorrow within him. He worked late trying to lift the sole responsibility from Mariana's shoulders. Mariana would often beg him to get his quota of sleep, to rest his weary body or to exchange his threadbare suit for a new one, but to no avail; he lived in another world. In art he was evolving a mode of expression that made the great Rodin call him at a later day, "The American Blake." In Arabic his contributions to the Arabian press of New York were copied by the press in the East, and Gibran, the youth lost in a world not of his making, was praised and criticized beyond the deserts of his years.

Their living was precarious as Mariana sewed and Gibran wrote. But Arabic literature yielded little or no money. Through his other talents for drawing and painting he made small sums; he designed book covers

and posed for other artists and was paid in paints—he sold a few drawings and labored steadily with pencil and brush in the hope of finally exhibiting a body of work in their universal language. By early 1904 he had more than twenty drawings to offer.

No gallery would receive his imaginative, mystical little pictures—great in spirit, small in size—but a poetic and independent photographer of Boston, who knew and loved the young man, opened his studio for the little exhibition. Gibran slaved feverishly in preparation, and the travail of his spirit when at last his pictures were on view is easier to imagine than to describe. There was a fair number of visitors who criticized or laughed, or praised, or were indifferent but no one even asked the price or evinced any great interest, and his spirit, so sorely tried by death, grew even more tender as he shrank into a corner.

Among all these spectators came one woman to whom the imaginative and religious quality in Gibran's work especially appealed. Sensing her interest, he offered to

explain his allegories, and their acquaintance ripened into a rare friendship. Her self-contained soul proved to be a spiritual and moral refuge and anchor for Gibran. She prevailed upon him to accept her aid and to go abroad for study; she encouraged him to write English and assisted him to a better understanding of this language. For the remainder of his life he had no closer friend than Mary Haskell. Barbara Young, the American poetess, who worked with Gibran from 1925 on, related to this writer that Gibran never submitted a line to his publishers without obtaining the final approval of Mary Haskell. His will bequeathed to this friend of his youth and manhood all the contents of his studio, and after placing some of his wash-drawings in the Metropolitan Museum of Fine Arts (New York), some in the Fogg Museum, Cambridge, Mass., some in the Boston Museum of Fine Arts and a few elsewhere, this friend sent all the remainder with the furnishings of his studio to his native Bcherri for his memorial in the old Monastery of Mar-Sarkis, where the

great body of his work remains on public view—a perpetual monument to his personality and genius.

From 1908 to 1910 Gibran worked at his art in Paris under the guidance of older artists, thence he returned to Boston, but in 1912 moved to New York, where he lived for the rest of his life in the old red "Studio Building" at 51 West 10th Street.

During the first ten years of his life in New York—the period of the World War—the fame and leadership of Gibran in the Arabic-speaking world grew steadily, spreading from North America to South America and to the Near East. While this Arabic world learned to recognize him as painter as well as writer, the English-speaking world became aware that he was a writer as well as a painter. In 1918, at the age of thirty-five, he summed up his meditations and philosophy in "The Processions" expressed in Arabic verse. "The Processions" was the precursor of and ripened into his English "Prophet" at the age of forty. In 1919 he published his first work in English, "The Madman"; "The

Forerunner" followed in 1920; and in 1923 his masterpiece, "The Prophet." On "The Prophet," the ultimate expression of his life, Gibran had worked many years. Beautiful in form, creative in thought, it found immediate and lasting favor, ranked among the classics of contemporary English literature; while "The Processions" translated here is his *opus magnus* in Arabic poetry.

Gibran had never been robust and from childhood he had suffered much. Although he could not banish pain, he toiled unceasingly and so whipped his body to writing and painting that he accomplished a giant's task. In New York he was thrown into the maelstrom of a mechanical age and an alien atmosphere. He used to shut himself up in his cloistral studio and rebelliously fight fate and circumstances, using his brush as a sword and his pen as a lance until battered and weary he passed out of the towering canyons into the smiling sunshine of Washington Street in lower New York within sight of the skyscrapers, where at every step a greeting in the musical Arabic was directed

to him and a hand was extended to welcome him. Here in the atmosphere of his native land he gathered with his fellow poets (the "Bards" of Washington Street) and sympathetic countrymen, to be transported into another world. For the five years following the publication of "The Prophet" he was at the summit of his fame and productiveness. In 1926 he published "Son of Man." Upon this book as much as upon "The Prophet" Gibran had worked since youth. The two were the very essence of his being, and in them he felt himself essentially fulfilled.

Gibran, who always longed for the freedom of Wadi-Quadisha, had started negotiations for the purchase of Mar-Sarkis, the deserted monastery. Now was the time to rest that weary body and sensitive soul that had soared so high and battled so valiantly. But poor Gibran was caught in the wreckage of the false things he had demolished; fame and wealth begot further obligations and further taxed his strength. Although he refused to leave his cloister in Greenwich Village for long, at last he realized that, aside

from a weakened heart, a fatal ailment was gnawing at his body. Not a word of complaint did he utter to his most intimate friends nor did he take a step to obtain relief. Sensing that he had reached the bend in the road, he stayed in his cloister and suffered but continued to work. So he wrote, sketched and suffered silence as became a soul which wished to rise above pain and suffering. On April 9, 1931, a friend came to see him and found him wracked by pain and wan from illness, yet still smiling wistfully like a brave child. He did not wish to be removed to a hospital; he wished to die in his cloister with his easel, paint and brushes, surrounded by his papers and books. Next morning he was taken to the hospital where he died on April 10, 1931, at the age of forty-eight.

It remained for the heartbroken Mariana to bring her beloved brother back to his native land and lay him to rest in the rock-hewn chapel of Mar-Sarkis, the deserted monastery he so longed for. The seaport of Beirut has never witnessed such a reception or funeral cortège. People from all over

Syria flocked to pay their respects to her gentle and gifted son.

Mountaineers from the hills and valleys deserted their villages and came chanting their funeral dirge while their companions joined them in the refrain. All the notables of the country were present to receive him, but this day was not the day of the notables, for Gibran recognized no notables. He belonged to the people and the people poured forth to meet him. The men and youth of Wadi-Quadisha went down to the seashore to claim their own and to bear him back to his birthplace. All along the road from near and distant villages streamed the women to greet the cortège at every cross-road. They came in groups headed by the waking (nadi-bat) women who lamented their beloved son. Youthful maidens wore their colorful kerchiefs and strewed the road with armfuls of native flowers, chanting and lamenting the passing of Tammuz.

المواكب

الشيخ

وليس يرضى بها غير الالى مكروا	الارض خبّارةٌ والدهر صاحبها
رهن الهوى وعلى التخدير قد فطروا	فالناس ان هربوا سرّوا كأنهم
اثرى وذلـك بالأحلام يختمر	هذا يعربـد ان صحّى وذاك اذا
تأتيه عفوًا ولم يحكم به الضجر	وقلّ في الارض من يرضى الحياة كما
اكواب وهم اذا طافوا بها خدروا	لذاك قد حوّلوا نهر الحياة الى
هل استظلّ بغيم ممطر قمر	فان رأيت اخا صحو فقل عجبا

الفتى

من مـدام أو خيـال	ليس في الغـابات سكر
غير اكسير الغمـام	فالسواقي ليس فيهـا
وحليبٌ للأنـام	انما التخـدير ثديٌّ
بلغوا من الفطـام	فاذا شاخوا ومـاتوا
فالفنـا خير الشراب	اعطني النـاي وغنّ
بعد ان تفنى الهضـاب	واين النـاي يبقى

الشيخ

والشر في الناس لا يفنى وان قبروا	الخير في الناس مصنوع اذا جُبروا
اصابع الدهر يومـا ثم تنكسر	فاكثر النـاس آلاتٌ تحركهـا
ولا تقول ذاك السيـد الوقر	فلا تقولن هذا عـالـم علمٌ
صوت الرعاة ومن لم يمش يندثر	فأفضل الناس قطعان يسير بها

(١)

الفتى

ليس في الغـــابات راع   لا ولا فيهـــا القطيع
فالثنــا يمشي ولكــن   لا يجـاريه الربيع
أعطني النــاي وغنّ   فالغنا يرعى العقول
وانين النــاي أبقى   من مجيد وذليـــل

الشيخ

وما الحيــاة سوى نوم تراوده   احلام من سراد النفس يا ستر
والسرّ في النفس حزن النفس يستره   فان توشى فبالافراح يستتر

الفتى

ليس في الغــابات حزن   لا ولا فيهـا الهموم
فاذا هبّ نسيـــم   لم تحي معه الغـــموم
أعطني النــاي وغنّ   فالغنا يمحو المحن
وانين النــاي يبقى   بعد أن يفنى الزمن

الشيخ

والدين في الناس حقل ليس يزرعه   غير الأنى لهم في زرعه وطـر
من آمل بنعيم الغله مبتشر   ومن جهول يخاف النــار تستعر
فالقوم لولا عقاب البعث ما عبدوا   ربا ولولا الثواب انرتجى كفروا
كأنما الدين غرب من متاجرهم   ان واظبوا ربحوا او اهملوا خسروا

الفتى

ليس في الغــابات دين   لا ولا الكفر القبيــح
فاذا البلبل غنى   لم يقل هذا الصحيح
ان دين الناس يأتي   مثل طـــل ويروح
لم يقم في الأرض دين   بعد طه والمسيح

الشيخ

به ويستضحك الاموات لو نظروا	والعدل في الارض يبكي الجن لو سمعوا
والمجد والفخر والاثراء ان كبروا	والسجن والموت للجانين ان صغروا
وسارق الحقل يدعى الباسل الخطر	فارق الزهـــر مذموم ومحتقر
وقاتل الروح لا تدري به البشر	وقاتل الجسم مقتول بفعلته

الفتى

لا ولا فيهــا العقـاب	ليس في الغابات عدل
ظلّــه فوق التراب	فاذا الصفصــاف ألقى
بدعة ضـدّ الكتاب	لا يقول السرو هـذي
ان رأتــه الشمس ذاب	ان عدل النـاس ثلج
فالغنا عدل القلـوب	اعطني النـاي وغنّ
بعد ان تفنى الذنـوب	وأنين النــاي يبقى

الشيخ

سادت وان ضعفت حلّت بها الغير	والحق للعزم والارواح ان قويت
عزم السواعد شاء الناس ام نكروا	والعزم في الروح حق ليس ينكره
قوم اذا ما رأوا اشبـاحهم نفروا	فان رأيت ضعيفـا سائدا فعلى
بنو الثعالب غاب الأسد ام حضروا	ففي العرينة ديج ليس يقربها
وفي البزاة شموخ وهي تحتضر	وهي الزرازير جبن وهي طــائرة

الفتى

لا ولا فيهـا الضعيف	ليس في الغــابات عزم
لم تقل هــذا المخيف	فاذا ما الأسد صاحت
في فضـا الفكر يطوف	ان عزم الناس ظل
مثل أوراق الخـريف	وحقوق الناس تبلى
فالغنا عزم النفوس	اعطني النـاي وغنّ
بعد ان تفنى الشمـوس	وانين النــاي يبقى

(٣)

الشيخ

والعلم في الناس سبلٌ بان أوّلها أمّا اواخرها فالدهر والقدر
وأفضل العلم حلمٌ ان ظفرت بـه وسرتَ ما بين ابناء الكرى سخروا
فان رأيت اخـا الاحلام منفرداً عن قومه وهو منبوذٌ ومحتقـرٌ
فهو النبيّ وبرد الغـد يحجبه عن امة برداء الامس تأتزرُ
وهو الغريب عن الدنيا وساكنها وهو المجاهر لام الناس او عذروا
وهو الشديد وان ابدى ملاينـةً وهو البعيد وان تدانى الناس ام هجروا

الفتى

ان علم النـاس طرّاً كضبـاب في الحقـول
فاذا الشمس أطلّت من ورا الافق يـزول

الشيخ

والحرُّ في الارض يبني من منازعه سجناً له وهو لا يـدري فيوثرُ
فان تحرّر من ابنـاء بجدتـه يظلّ عبدا لمن يهوى ويفتكـر

الفتى

ليس في الغـابات حرٌّ لا ولا العبـد الذميم
انما الامجاد سخفٌ وفقـاقيعٌ تعـوم
فاذا ما اللوزُ الهى زهره فوق الهشيم
لم يقل هــذا صغيرٌ وانا المـولى الكريم

الشيخ

واللطف في الناس اهداف وان نمت اضلاعها لم تكن في جوفها الدررُ
فان لقيت قويّـاً لينـا فبـه لأعين فقـدتْ ابصارها البصر

(٤)

الفتى

لـه لـين' الجبـان'	ليـس في الغـاب لطيـف'
في جـوار النـديان	ففصـون' البـان تعلـو
كـالأرجـوان	واذا الطـاووس أعطـى حلـــة'
فيـه ام فيـه افتتـان	فهـو لا يــدري أحسـن'
فالغنـا لطـف' الوديـع	اعطنـي النـــاي وغـن'
مـن ضيـف وفليــح	وانيـن النبـاي أبقـى

الشيخ

ننسـى المجانيـن حتـى يغـر الغمـر'	وقـل' نسينـا الفـاتحيـن ومـا
وفـي حشـاشـة قيـس هيـكـل' وقـر'	قـدكان في قلـب ذي القرنيـن مجـزرة'
وفـي انكـارات هـذا الفـوز' والظغـر'	فغـي انتصـارات هـذا غلبـة' خفيـت'
كـالغمـر للـوحي لا للكـر ينصـر'	والحـب في الـروح لا في الجسـم نعرفـه

الفتى

غيـر ذكـر العـاشقيـن'	ليـس في الغـابـات ذكـر'
وطفـوا بالعـالميـن	فالأولـى مـادوا ومـادوا
في أسـامي المجرميـن	اصبحـوا مثـل حـروف
عنـدنـا الغتـح المبيـن	فالهـوى الغضــاح يدعـى

الشيخ

في جـوعـه شبـع' وفي ورده الصـدر'	فـان لقيـت' محبـا هائمـا كلفـاً
يبغـي مـن الحـب اذ يرجـو فيططـر'	والنـاس قـالوا هـو المجنـون مـاذا عسـى
وليـس في تلك مـا يحلـو ويعتبـر'	افـي هـوى تلـك يستـدمي محـاجـره'
أنـى درواكـه' مـن يحـى ومـا اختبـروا	فغـل هـم البهـم' مـاتوا قبـل مـا ولـدوا

(٥)

الفتى

لا ولا فيهــا الرقيب	ليس في الغابات عــذلٌ
اذ ترى وجـــه المغيب	فاذا الغـــزلان جُنّـت
انّ ذا شيءٌ عجيب	لا يقول النسرُ واهـــاً
عندنا الأمر الغـــريب	انا العـــاقل يُدعى

الشيخ

يرجى فان مار جسـا مكُ البشرْ	وما السعادة في الدنيـا سوى شبح
حتى اذا جــاءه يبطي ويتكسـر	كالنهر يركض نحو السهل مكتدحاً
الى المنيع فان صــاروا به فتروا	لم يسعد الناسُ الاّ في تشوّقهم
عن المنيع فقل في خُلْقه البشر	فان لقيت سعيداً وهو منصرفٌ

الفتى

لا ولا فيـه الملـل	ليس في الغاب رجــاءٌ
وعلى الكلّ حصـل	كيف يرجو الغاب جزءاً
أمــلاً وهـو الأمل	وبمـا السعيُ يغـاب
احدى هاتيك العلـل	انا العيش رجــاءٌ
فالغنـا نارٌ ونـورٌ	اعطني الناي وغنّ
لا يُــدانيه الغتـور	وأنيــس النــاي شوقٌ

الشيخ

فلا المظاهر تبديهـا ولا الصورُ	وغاية الروح طيّ الروح قد خفيت
حدُّ الكمـال تلاشت وانقضى الخبر	فذا يقول هي الأرواح ان بلغت
ومرّت الريح يوما عــافها الشجر	كأنّما هي اثمـارٌ اذا نضجت
لم يبقَ في الروح نهويمٌ ولا سمر	وذا يقــول هي الأجسام ان هجمت
تعكر المــاء ولّت وامّحى الأثر	كأنّما هي ظلٌّ في الغدير اذا
تثوى ولا هي في الأرواح تختضر	كلُّ الجميعُ فلا الذرّات في جسمه
الاّ ومرّةً بهــا الشرقي فتنتشر	فما طوت شمالٌ اذيال عـاقلة

(٦)

الفتى

بيـــن نفسي وجـــودٌ	لم اجد في الغاب فرقاً
والنــدى مـــاءٌ ركد	فالهـــوا ماءٌ تهـــادى
والشرى زهرٌ حسـد	والشَّذا زهرٌ تمـــادى
ظنَّ ليلا فرقـــد	وظلال الحور حـــورٌ

الشيخ

حتى البلـــوغ فتستعلي وينفصم	والجسم للروح رحمٌ تستكنُّ بـه
عهد المخـاض فلا سقطٌ ولا عسر	فهي الجنين وما يوم الحمام سوى
عقمُ القسيّ التي ما شدّهــا وتر	لكنَّ في الناس اشباحا يلازمهـا
من القفيل ولم يحبل بها البدر	فهي الدخيلة والارواح ما وُلـدت

الفتى

لا ولا فيهـــا الدخيل	ليس في الغـــاب عقيمٌ
حفظت سرَّ النخيـــل	انّ في التمـــر نواةٌ
عـن قفير وحقـــول	وبقرص الشهـد رمزٌ
صيغ من معنى الخمـول	انا العصـــاقرُ لفظٌ
فالفنـا جسمٌ يسيـــل	أعطني النـــاي وغنِّ
من مسـوخ ونغـول	وأنينُ النـــاي ابقى

الشيخ

ولانيري فهـو البدء والظفـر	والموت في الارض لابن الارض خاتمة
يبقى ومن نام كل الليـل يندثر	فمن يعانق في احلامه سحـــرا
يعانق الترب حتى تخمد الزهـر	ومن يلازم تربا حال يقظتــه
يجتازه ، واخو الاثقال ينحــدر	فالموت كالبحر من خفّت عناصره

الفتى

لا ولا فيها القبـور	ليس في الغابات موتٌ
لم يمت نعمـه السرور .	فاذا نيسانُ ولـــّى
ينثني طيَّ الصـــدور	ان هول المـــوت وهمٌ
كالذي عـاش الدهور	فالّذي عاش ربيعـــا
فالفنـا سرُّ الخلـود	أعطني النـــاي وغنِّ
بعد ان يفنى الوجود	وأنيـــنُ النـــاي يبقى

الفتى

أعطني النـاي وغنّ	وانس ما قلت وقلتـا
اثما النطق هبـاء	فاُفـدني ما فعلتـا
هل تخذت الغاب مثلي	منزلاً دون القصـور
فتتبعت الـسواقي	وتسلّقت الصخـور
هل تحممت بطـر	وتنشّقت بنـور
وشربت الفجـر خمرا	في كؤوس من اثيـر
هل جلست الصبح مثلي	بين جفنـات العنب
والعناقيـد تدلّت	كريـّات الـذهب
هل فرشت العشب ليـلا	وتلحّفت الفضـا
زاهدا في ما سيأتي	نائيا ما قـد مضى
وسكوت الليـل بحر	موجـه في مسمعـك
ويصـدر الليل قلب	خـافق في مضجعـك
أعطني النـاي وغنّ	وانس داء ودواء
انما الناس سطور	كتبت لكـنْ بماء
ليت شعري أي نفح	في اجتمـاع وزحـام
وجـدال وضجيـج	واحتجـاج وخصـام
كلها انفاق خلـد	وخيـوط العنكبـوت
فالـذي يحيى بعجـز	فهـو في بطء يـموت

الشيخ

العيش في الغاب والايام لو نُظمت	في قبضتي لغدت في الغاب تنتثر
لكن هو الدهر في نفسي له أرب	فكلّما رمت غابـاً قام يعتـذر
وللتقـادير سبل لا تغيّرهـا	والناس في عجزهم عن قصدهم قصرواً

(٨)

The Procession of Gibran

In 1919 Gibran surprised his friends by issuing at his own expense, a beautiful and artistic book containing "The Procession"—his hidden masterpiece of Arabic poetry. The paper, the type, illustrations and binding all bespoke the tender regard and care that Gibran had bestowed upon this unique child.

The Arabic is a forceful language with a prolific vocabulary of pregnant words of fine shadings. Its delicate tones of warmth and color form with its melodies a symphony, the sound of which moves its listeners to tears or ecstasy. Anyone present at an Arabian gathering where prose or poetry is recited may readily note how the heads and then the bodies of the listeners commence to sway in rhythmic accompaniment to the recitation. In "The Procession" we often find Gibran carried away by the charm of the lyric and oblivious to the strict continuity in the Kasida.

Nassib 'Arida, the gifted Arabian poet,

wrote the introduction to "The Procession" and explained how the dual discourse came about:

"An old sage, worldly-wise and ripened by experience, had left the city to wander in the countryside, and wearily rested himself at the edge of the forest; a naked, sun-bronzed youth emerged from the forest, reed in hand, to throw himself in abandon beside the sage, and the two unceremoniously commenced their discourse."

The sage pours forth his wisdom in measured logic and a tinge of disappointment while the rebellious youth bursts out with his expressions of the Universality of the Whole.

To this translator, the poem represents the unconscious autobiography of Gibran: Gibran the sage, mellowed beyond his years, and Gibran the rebel, who had come to believe in the Unity and Universality of all existence and who longed for simple, impersonal freedom, merged in harmony with all things.

I feel that it does not behoove one to

venture into a critical study of the poem but rather to permit each reader to quaff according to his own cup—his intellectual and emotional capacity. For Gibran himself, a master of both the pen and brush, finds these mediums inadequate: at the end of each refrain he takes refuge in the non-dimensional, limitless medium—the plaint of the reed—or spiritual essence.

Those who read Gibran's life and knew of his yearning for the peace of Wadi-Quadisha and Mar-Sarkis can now read the philosophy of the rebellious child of nature in the following:

Give to me the reed and sing thou!
   Forget all the cures and ills;
Mankind is like verses written
   Upon the surface of the rills.
What good is there, pray thee tell me
   In jostling through the crowd in life
'Mid the argumental tumult,
   Protestation, and endless strife,
Mole-like burrowing in darkness,

Grasping for the spider's thread,
　　Always thwarted in ambition
　　　　Until the living join the dead?

And the humane, wounded and battered
Gibran, with a tinge of resignation, foretells
the end:

Had I the days in hand to string,
　　Only in forest they'd be strewn,
But circumstances drive us on
　　In narrow paths by Kismet hewn.
For Fate has ways we cannot change
　　While weakness preys upon our Will.
We bolster with excuse the self,
　　And help that Fate ourselves to kill.

G. KHEIRALLAH

THE ILLUSORY WORLD

SAGE

This world is but a winery,
   Its host and master Father Time,
Who caters only to those steep'd
   In dreams discordant, without rhyme.

For people drink and race as though
   They were the steeds of mad desire;
Thus some are blatant when they pray,
   And others frenzied to acquire.

Few on this earth who savor life,
   And are not bor'd by its free gifts;
Or divert not its streams to cups
   In which their fancy floats and drifts.

Should you then find a sober soul
   Amidst this state of revelry,
Marvel how a moon did find
   In this rain cloud a canopy.

YOUTH

No confusion in the forest
   From illusion or from wine,
For the clouds endow the brooklet
   With elixir superfine.

Yet the human turns to drugging,
   As to nursing from the breast;
Coming to the age of weaning
   Only when he's put to rest.

Give to me the reed and sing thou!
   For the song is gracious shade,
And the plaint of reed remaineth
   When illusions dim and fade.

OF GOODNESS AND STATION

SAGE

The good in man should freely flow,
    As evil lives beyond the grave;
While Time with fingers moves the pawns
    Awhile, then breaks the knight and knave.

Say not, "There goes a learned man"
    Nor, "There a chieftain dignified."
The best of men are in the herd,
    And heed the shepherd as their guide.

YOUTH

In the forest no one shepherds,
    Nor the flocks are culled apart,
Spring and Winter are not rivals,
    Each in season plays its part.

Give to me the reed and sing thou!
    For the song shepherds the mind,
And the reed's plaint is more lasting
    Than the ranks of humankind.

OF LIFE AND SORROW

SAGE

Life is but a sleep disturbed
  By dreaming, prompted by the will;
The saddened soul with sadness hides
  Its secrets, and the gay, with thrill.

YOUTH

In the forest no one sorrows,
  Nor is one downcast by grief.
Zephyrs carry but compassion
  When they whisper to the leaf.

Give to me the reed and sing thou!
  Let the song erase the sorrow,
For the plaint of reed remaineth,
  When the past rejoins the morrow.

OF RELIGION

SAGE

Religion is a well-tilled field,
    Planted and watered by desire
Of one who longed for Paradise,
    Or one who dreaded Hell and Fire.

Aye, were it but for reckoning
    At Resurrection, they had not
Worshipped God, nor did repent,
    Except to gain a better lot—

As though religion were a phase
    Of commerce in their daily trade;
Should they neglect it they would lose—
    Or persevering would be paid.

YOUTH

In the wild there is no Credo
   Nor a hideous disbelief;
Song-birds never are assertive
   Of the Truth, the Bliss, or Grief.

People's creeds come forth, then perish
   Like the shadows in the night.
No faith stood out after Taha's*
   And the Christ to shed its light.

* Taha, the Prophet Muhammed.

OF JUSTICE

SAGE

Justice on earth would cause the Jinn
  To cry at misuse of the word,
And were the dead to witness it,
  They'd mock at fairness in this world.

Yea, death and prison we mete out
  To small offenders of the laws,
While honor, wealth, and full respect
  On greater pirates we bestow.

To steal a flower we call mean,
  To rob a field is chivalry;
Who kills the body he must die,
  Who kills the spirit he goes free.

YOUTH

In the wild there is no justice
   Nor is there a punishment.
When the willows cast their shadow
   O'er the ground without consent,

No one hears the cypress saying,
   "This act is versus law and right."
Like the snow, our Human Justice
   Melts from shame in warm sunlight!

Give to me the reed and sing thou!
   Song to heart is judge sublime,
And the plaint of reed remaineth
   After the end of guilt and crime.

OF WILL AND RIGHT

SAGE

To Will belongs the Right. For Souls
 When strong prevail, when weak become
Subject to changes, good and bad,
 And with the wind may go and come.

Then, deny not that Will in Soul
 Is greater than the Might of Arm,
And weakling only mounts the throne
 Of those beyond the good and harm.

Lo! in the lion's lair a scent
 Which bids the fox's cubs away,
Whether the denizens are there,
 Or in the forest on foray.

And thus it is with certain birds
 Who, though on wing in the free space
Are ever frightened by the hawk,
 Who, dying, keeps his pride of race.

Youth

Nature tolerates no weakling,
  Nor permits the wilful sway.
When the lions roar their presence
  Forest does not feel dismay.

Man's will is a floating shadow
  In the mind that he conceives,
And the rights of mankind pass and
  Perish like the Autumn leaves.

Give to me the reed and sing thou!
  Song imparts to Soul a Will,
And the plaint of reed remaineth
  When the suns are dark and still.

OF SCIENCE AND KNOWLEDGE

SAGE

Learning follows various roads.
   We note the start but not the end.
For Time and Fate must rule the course,
   While we see not beyond the bend.

The best of knowledge is a dream
   The gainer holds steadfast, uncowed
By ridicule, and moves serene,
   Despised and lowly in the crowd.

Such is the Prophet, who arrives
   Veiled in the cloak of future thought,
'Mid people hid in ancient garb,
   Who could not see the gift he brought.

He is a stranger to this life,
   Stranger to those who praise or blame,
For he upholds the Torch of Truth,
   Although devoured by the flame.

He is the strong, although he seems
    Gentle and meek in ev'ry way.
He is remote from those who are
    Quite near to him, or far away.

YOUTH

Present knowledge of the people
    Is a fog above the field;
When the sun mounts the horizon
    To its rays the mist will yield.

OF FREEDOM

SAGE

The free on earth builds of his strife
  A prison for his own duress,
When he is freed from his own kin,
  Is slave to thought and love's caress.

YOUTH

In the forest dwells no freeman,
  Nor is there a humble slave.
Honors are but false delusions,
  Like the froth upon the wave.

Should the almond spray its blossoms
  On the turf around its feet,
Never will it claim a lordship,
  Nor disdain the grass to greet.

OF HAPPINESS AND HOPE

Sage

Happiness is a myth we seek,
  If manifested surely irks;
Like river speeding to the plain,
  On its arrival slows and murks.

For man is happy only in
  His aspiration to the heights;
When he attains his goal, he cools
  And longs for other distant flights.

If you should meet a happy one
  Who is contented with his lot,
Unlike the rest of all mankind,
  Pray his Nirvana disturb not.

YOUTH

Hope is found not in the forest,
  Nor the wild portray despair;
Why should forest long for portions
  When the ALL is centered there?

Should one search the forest hopeful,
  When *all nature* is the Aim?
For to hope is but an ailment,
  So are station, wealth and fame.

Give to me the reed and sing thou!
  For the song is flame and light,
And the reed's plaint is a yearning
  Unattained by lazy wight.

OF GENTLENESS

SAGE

The gentleness of some is like
  A polished shell with silky feel,
Lacking the precious pearl within,
  Oblivious of the brother's weal.

When you shall meet one who is strong
  And gentle too, pray feast your eyes;
For he is glorious to behold,
  The blind can see his qualities.

YOUTH

No one in the wild is gentle,
  Pliant, shrinking like a coward.
There, the slender reed and oak tree
  Side by side are striving upward.

If the peacock there is given
    Purple raiment to fore-arm,
It is unaware of beauty,
    And unconscious of the charm.

Give to me the reed and sing thou!
    For the song comforts the meek,
And the plaint of reed remaineth
    Longer than the strong and weak.

OF LOVE

SAGE

Forgotten is the glory of
   The intrepid Conquistadors,
But never 'til the end of time
   Will we forget the paramours!

For in Macedonian's heart
   We picture but a slaughter-house.
While in the heart of Qais we paint*
   A Rever'd Temple to espouse.

And in the triumph of the first
   We find an ignoble defeat,
While in the foiling of the last
   The victory became complete.

For love lies in the soul alone,
   Not in the body, and like wine
Should stimulate our better self
   To welcome gifts of Love Divine.

* Qais, Majnun Laila (the bewitched of Laila), the
ideal lover of the Arabs.

YOUTH

In the forest there is mention
  But of those who madly love;
As to Kings who ruled and lorded,
  And oppress'd from thrones above,—

They are but as faded letters
  In the pages of their crime;
Raging passion in its season
  Through the forest reigns sublime.

OF LOVE

SAGE

Now should you meet a lover lost,
   Bewildered, yet avoiding guide,
Disdaining though he thirsts to drink,
   In his own hunger satisfied;

Hear people say, "This youth bewitched
   "What seek he from a love so great?
"What hope has he to patiently
   "Await his Kismet and his Fate?

"Why waste his bloodstained tears for one
   "Who lacks all beauty and respect?"
Say of them all, they are stillborn,
   Know naught of life, nor can reflect.

YOUTH

In the woods no blame attaches
    To lover's tryst, nor watchers spy;
When a gazelle, ranging swiftly,
    Greets its lovemate with a cry,

Eagles never display wonder,
    Or say, "'Tis marvel of the age."
For in nature we the children
    Only hold the sane as strange.

OF SOUL AND FERTILITY

SAGE

The reason why the soul exists
　　Is folded in the soul itself;
No painting could its essence show,
　　Nor manifest its real self.

Some say when the souls do reach
　　Perfection, then they merge in nil,
As though they were the ripened fruit
　　Dropp'd from the tree by wind and chill.

While others claim the body is
　　The *all-in-all*, and at the break
The soul or mind existing not
　　Will slumber not, nor will awake.

As though the soul were shadow frail
　　Reflected in a brooklet clear,
To be erased whene'er the stream
　　Is mirked, and forthwith disappear.

All are mistaken, for the spark
    Shall perish not with form or soul;
For whatever North Wind foldeth,
    East Wind passing will unroll.

YOUTH

In the forest no distinction
    Of soul or body is instilled.
Air is water aerated,
    And the dew—water distilled.

Fragrance is but bloom extended;
    Earth is blossoms frozen deep;
Shade of poplars—only houris*
    Thought it night and fell asleep.

* or poplars

OF SOUL AND FERTILITY

SAGE

The body is a womb to soul
In which it dwells until full term,
When it ascends once more to soar,
While womb again recedes to germ.

The soul a babe, and day of fate
Is day of birth without mishap,
But some are ever sterile and
Unbending as the bows that snap.

Such intruders give no birth,
For souls are not the fruit of tree
Which long has dried; and baked clay
Never begot the THEE and ME.

YOUTH

Nature tolerates no barren
   Nor intruder without qualm.
Aye! the pit in date has guarded
   All the secrets of the palm,

And the honeycomb is symbol
   Of the hive and of the field;
Sterile is a letter borrowed
   From "Ineptitude to yield."

Give to me the reed and sing thou!
   For the song is flowing form,
And the plaint of reed remaineth
   When the wry and odd conform.

OF DEATH AND IMMORTALITY

SAGE

And death on earth, to son of earth
  Is final, but to him who is
Ethereal, it is but the start
  Of triumph certain to be his.

If one embraces dawn in dreams,
  He is immortal! Should he sleep
His long night through, he surely fades
  Into a sea of slumber deep.

For he who closely hugs the ground
  When wide awake will crawl 'til end.
And death, like sea, who braves it light
  Will cross it. Weighted will descend.

YOUTH

There is not a death in nature,
  Nor a grave is set apart;
Should the month of April vanish
  "Gifts of joy" do not depart.

Fear of death is a delusion
  Harbored in the breast of sages;
He who lives a single Springtime
  Is like one who lives for ages.

Give to me the reed and sing thou!
  For song is Immortality,
And the plaint of reed remaineth
  After the joy and misery.

THE SUMMING OF THE YOUTH

Give to me the reed and sing thou!
  Forget hence what both have stated;
Words are but the motes in rainbow,
  Tell me now of joys you've tasted.

Have you taken to the forest,
  Shunned the palace for abode?
Followed brooklets in their courses,
  Climbed the rocks along the road?

Have you ever bathed in fragrance,
  Dried yourself in sheets of light?
Ever quaff the wine of dawning,
  From ethereal goblets bright?

Have you rested at the sunset,
  As I have beneath the vine?
Laden with suspended clusters,
  Ripened to golden crystalline?

Ever bedded in the herbage,
  Quilted by a heavenly vast,
Unconcerned about the future,
  And forgetful of your past?

Felt that the nocturnal silence,
  Sea-like surged around your head,
That the breast of night had harbored
  A throbbing heart within your bed?

Give to me the reed and sing thou!
  Forget all the cures and ills,
Mankind is like verses written
  Upon the surface of the rills.

What good is there, pray thee tell me,
  In jostling through the crowd in life,
'Mid the argumental tumult,
  Protestation, and endless strife;

Mole-like burrowing in darkness,
  Grasping for the spider's thread,
Always thwarted in ambition,
  Until the living join the dead?

THE CAPITULATION OF THE SAGE

Had I the days in hand to string,
    Only in forest they'd be strewn,
But circumstances drive us on
    In narrow paths by Kismet hewn.

For Fate has ways we cannot change,
    While weakness preys upon our Will;
We bolster with excuse the self,
    And help that Fate ourselves to kill.